Table of Contents

Resilient Voices:
A Poetry Anthology

Anthology Introduction

In a world filled with challenges, joys, sorrows, and triumphs, the power of poetry lies in its ability to capture the essence of human experience. ***Resilient Voices: A Poetry Anthology*** is more than just a collection of verses—it's a celebration of the strength, hope, and resilience that reside within each of us.

This anthology brings together the evocative work of Narrato Insights, combining two beloved poetry collections, "Welcome to Flourish" and "Echoes of Unity", that have touched readers around the globe. These poems speak to the soul, offering comfort in times of need, inspiration when hope seems distant, and a sense of connection that transcends the barriers of time and space.

The poems within these pages are born from the depths of human experience. They explore themes of love, loss, perseverance, and renewal, reminding us that we are never truly alone in our journey. Each piece is a testament to the indomitable spirit that drives us to overcome, to rise, and to flourish, no matter the obstacles we face.

As you turn these pages, you will find words that resonate with your own story, that echo your struggles, your triumphs, and your dreams. ***Resilient Voices*** is an invitation to reflect, to heal, and to find strength in the shared experiences of others. It is a reminder that within every heart beats the potential for greatness, and within every mind lies the power to overcome.

We invite you to immerse yourself in this anthology, to find your voice within its lines, and to carry its message of hope and resilience with you. Whether you are seeking solace, inspiration, or simply a moment of peace, may these poems speak to you, uplift you, and remind you of the beauty that lies within the human spirit.

Welcome to ***Resilient Voices: A Poetry Anthology***—a journey into the heart of what it means to be human.

Welcome to Flourish:
Inspirational Poems for Mental Wellness

Narrato Insights

INTRODUCTION

In a world that often feels rushed, chaotic, and overwhelming, finding moments of peace and inspiration can be a profound challenge. Yet, it is precisely in these moments of stillness and reflection that we discover the keys to our well-being and fulfillment. **Welcome to Flourish: Inspirational Poems for Mental Wellness**, a collection of poems crafted to nurture your soul, elevate your spirit, and guide you toward a life of balance, joy, and inner peace.

Finding Fulfillment in the Everyday

Fulfillment is not a distant goal, but a journey that unfolds in the present moment. It is found in the simple pleasures of everyday life—the warmth of the morning sun, the gentle rustle of leaves in the breeze, the laughter shared with loved ones, and the quiet moments of introspection. The poems in this collection invite you to pause and appreciate these small yet significant moments. They encourage you to slow down, breathe deeply, and immerse yourself in the beauty that surrounds you.

In our quest for fulfillment, it is essential to cultivate a mindset of gratitude. By acknowledging and appreciating the positive aspects of our lives, we shift our focus from what we lack to what we have. This shift in perspective can transform our outlook, making us more resilient in the face of challenges and more open to the abundance of joy that life has to offer.

Embracing Your Inner Strength

Each of us possesses a wellspring of inner strength, waiting to be tapped into. Life's trials and tribulations are opportunities to discover and harness this strength. The poems in **Flourish** remind you that resilience is not the absence of struggle, but the ability to rise above it. They celebrate the courage it takes to face adversity and the triumph of emerging stronger and wiser.

To truly flourish, it is vital to embrace vulnerability. Allowing yourself to be open and honest about your feelings creates a space for healing and growth. Vulnerability is not a sign of weakness; it is a testament to your authenticity and humanity. By accepting and expressing your true self, you pave the way for deeper connections and more meaningful experiences.

Nurturing Your Mind and Spirit

Mental wellness is a cornerstone of a fulfilling life. It encompasses our emotional, psychological, and social well-being, influencing how we think, feel, and act. The poems in this book serve as gentle reminders to prioritize your mental health, to take time for self-care, and to seek support when needed. They encourage you to practice mindfulness, to be present in the moment, and to engage in activities that bring you joy and peace.

Self-care is an essential practice for maintaining mental wellness. It involves setting boundaries, prioritizing rest, and engaging in activities that nourish your mind, body, and soul. The poems in Flourish inspire you to create a self-care routine that aligns with your needs and passions. Whether it's a walk in nature, a quiet moment of meditation, or immersing yourself in a creative hobby, self-care is a powerful tool for restoring balance and vitality.

The Power of Connection

Human connections are a vital source of support, love, and inspiration. The relationships we nurture have a profound impact on our mental wellness and overall fulfillment. Flourish emphasizes the importance of building and maintaining meaningful connections. It celebrates the joy of shared experiences, the comfort of companionship, and the strength found in community.

Reach out to loved ones, cultivate new friendships, and engage with your community. These connections enrich your life, providing a network of support and a sense of belonging. Remember, you are never alone in your journey; there are always people who care and are willing to walk alongside you.

A Journey of Continuous Growth

Life is a continuous journey of growth and self-discovery. The poems in this collection encourage you to embrace change, to learn from every experience, and to strive for personal growth. They remind you that every step, no matter how small, is a valuable part of your journey toward fulfillment.

<u>Gentle Resilience</u>

In the face of storms,
Stand firm and tall,
Gentle resilience,
Conquers all.

<u>Inner Sanctuary</u>

Find within,
Your sacred space,
An inner sanctuary,
A peaceful place.

<u>Healing Winds</u>

Winds of change,
Blow through the soul,
With healing whispers,
They make us whole.

<u>Unseen Strength</u>

Beneath the surface,
Lies a strength unseen,
In moments of struggle,
It's where you lean.

Silent Peace

In silent moments,
Peace can grow,
A quiet mind,
A tranquil flow.

Circle of Care

In circles warm with friendship's light,
Positive bonds will make things right.
Allow these ties that bind,
To nurture both your heart and mind.

Rise Above

When darkness falls,
Rise above,
With a heart full of hope,
And boundless love.

Silver Linings

In darkest clouds, seek silver light,
Hope and optimism in your sight.
Rest assured, a hopeful heart,
Can light your way, a brand new start.

Breath of Life

In every breath,
Find your calm,
A breath of life,
A healing balm.

A Ray of Hope

Even in shadows,
A ray of hope shines,
Guiding you forward,
Through uncertain times.

Boundless Possibilities

Life holds,
Boundless possibilities,
In each new day,
Find your abilities.

Bending Trees

Like trees that bend but do not break,
Resilience, for your own sake.
You will find this mental skill,
Helps you climb each daunting hill.

<u>Strength in Unity</u>
Together we stand,
Stronger than one,
In unity,
Our battles are won.

<u>Courageous Souls</u>
Courageous souls,
Fight battles unseen,
In their bravery,
True strength is gleaned.

<u>Finding Serenity</u>
In quiet moments,
Serenity lies,
A peaceful heart,
Under calm skies.

<u>Rise and Heal</u>
Rise from the ashes,
Heal from the pain,
In each new step,
Strength you'll gain.

A Gentle Light

Be a gentle light,
In someone's night,
With kindness and love,
Make their world bright.

Healing Journey

Walk the path,
Of healing and grace,
In every step,
Find your place.

Inner Harmony

Seek harmony,
Within your soul,
A balanced mind,
Makes you whole.

Heartfelt Words

Speak from the heart,
In words sincere,
In their truth,
Find your cheer.

<u>New Horizons</u>

Each horizon,
Holds new hope,
With every sunrise,
Learn to cope.

<u>Finding Joy</u>

Find joy in,
The little things,
In moments of peace,
Your heart sings.

<u>Silent Strength</u>

Strength in silence,
Is often found,
In quiet resolve,
Our hearts unbound.

<u>Grow Within</u>

Grow within, embrace your change,
Personal growth, a life arranged.
This path you take,
Brings wellness, every step you make.

<u>A Brighter Day</u>
Each new day,
Is a chance to mend,
With love and hope,
The heart will bend.

<u>The Healing Path</u>
Step by step,
On the healing path,
With love and support,
Escape the wrath.

<u>Brave New Dawn</u>
A new dawn breaks,
With brave intent,
In its light,
Find peace and content.

<u>Silent Guardian</u>
Be a silent guardian,
Of your own mind,
In your vigilance,
Peace you'll find.

<u>Inner Garden</u>
Tend to the garden,
Of your inner soul,
In its growth,
Find yourself whole.

<u>New Beginnings</u>
Every dawn,
Brings a new start,
A chance to heal,
A mending heart.

<u>Inner Strength</u>
Strength resides,
Within the soul,
Through trials and pain,
It makes us whole.

<u>Breaking Chains</u>
Break the chains,
That hold you back,
With each step forward,
You find the track.

Silent Tears

Silent tears,
Speak volumes loud,
In their release,
We stand unbowed.

Embracing Self

Embrace yourself,
With all your flaws,
In self-acceptance,
There are no laws.

Finding Light

In the darkness,
Seek the light,
A beacon of hope,
Burning bright.

Healing Words

Words of comfort,
Healing and kind,
Can ease the burden,
Of a troubled mind.

<u>Embrace Your Story</u>

Your story is yours,
With all its highs and lows,
Embrace it fully,
And let your courage show.

Conclusion

As we come to the end of **Welcome to Flourish: Inspirational Poems for Mental Wellness**, I hope these verses have touched your heart and provided you with moments of reflection, solace, and inspiration. This collection was created to be a companion on your journey towards mental wellness and fulfillment, reminding you of the inherent strength, beauty, and potential within you.

Embrace the Journey

Life is an ever-evolving journey filled with highs and lows, challenges and triumphs. The poems in this book encourage you to embrace every part of this journey with an open heart and a resilient spirit. Fulfillment is not found in a single moment or achievement, but in the continuous process of growth and self-discovery.

Remember that each step you take, no matter how small, is significant. Progress is not always linear, and setbacks are a natural part of the journey. What matters is your ability to rise, learn, and move forward with determination and grace. Celebrate your victories, learn from your challenges, and keep moving towards the life you envision.

Cultivate Mindfulness and Gratitude

One of the most powerful tools for achieving fulfillment is mindfulness—the practice of being present and fully engaged in the moment. By focusing on the here and now, you can appreciate the beauty of life's simplest pleasures and find peace amidst the chaos. The poems in Flourish invite you to pause, breathe, and savor these moments of tranquility and connection.

Gratitude is another cornerstone of a fulfilling life. By recognizing and appreciating the positive aspects of your life, you can shift your perspective from scarcity to abundance. Keep a gratitude journal, take time each day to reflect on what you are thankful for, and express your appreciation to those around you. Gratitude can transform your outlook, enhance your relationships, and bring a sense of contentment and joy.

Nurture Your Mental and Emotional Well-Being

Your mental and emotional well-being is essential for a fulfilling life. Prioritize self-care and make it a regular part of your routine. Self-care is not a luxury but a necessity, allowing you to recharge and maintain your overall health. Engage in activities that bring you joy, relaxation, and a sense of accomplishment.

Listen to your body and mind and give yourself permission to rest when needed. Practice mindfulness, meditation, or other relaxation techniques to reduce stress and cultivate inner peace. Seek professional help when necessary, and do not hesitate to reach out to friends and family for support. Remember, it's okay to ask for help and to take time for yourself.

Build Meaningful Connections

Human connections are vital for mental wellness and fulfillment. Surround yourself with people who uplift, support, and inspire you. Cultivate relationships that are based on mutual respect, understanding, and love. These connections provide a sense of belonging and a network of support that can help you navigate life's challenges.

Be present in your interactions, listen with empathy, and express your feelings openly and honestly. Building and maintaining meaningful relationships takes effort, but the rewards are immense. Engage in your community, participate in activities that align with your interests, and seek out opportunities to connect with others who share your values and passions.

Pursue Your Passions and Dreams

A fulfilling life is one where you pursue your passions and dreams with enthusiasm and dedication. Identify what brings you joy and fulfillment and make time for these activities in your daily life. Whether it's a hobby, a career goal, or a personal project, pursuing your passions can bring a deep sense of purpose and satisfaction.

Set realistic and achievable goals and break them down into manageable steps. Celebrate your progress, no matter how small, and stay motivated by reminding yourself of why you started. Stay open to new opportunities and be willing to adapt your plans as you grow and learn. Your passions and dreams are unique to you, and they are a vital part of your journey towards fulfillment.

Embrace Change and Growth

Change is an inevitable part of life and embracing it can lead to profound personal growth. View challenges as opportunities to learn and evolve. The poems in **Flourish** remind you that growth often comes from stepping out of your comfort zone and facing new experiences with courage and curiosity.

Reflect on your experiences, and use them as stepping stones towards becoming the best version of yourself. Personal growth is a lifelong process, and every experience, good or bad, contributes to your development. Embrace change with an open mind and a positive attitude, knowing that each step forward brings you closer to your goals.

Find Joy in the Present Moment

Ultimately, fulfillment is found in the present moment. By living mindfully and appreciating the here and now, you can experience a deeper sense of joy and contentment. Let go of past regrets and future anxieties and focus on the beauty and possibilities of the present.

Take time each day to do something that brings you happiness, whether it's spending time with loved ones, engaging in a favorite activity, or simply enjoying the quiet moments of life. The present moment is where life happens, and by fully embracing it, you can find true fulfillment and peace.

As you close the pages of **Flourish: Inspirational Poems for Mental Wellness,** carry the wisdom and inspiration of these poems with you. Let them serve as reminders of your strength, resilience, and the boundless potential within you. May they inspire you to embrace your journey with an open heart, to cultivate mindfulness and gratitude, and to pursue a life of joy, purpose, and fulfillment.

Thank you for allowing these poems to be a part of your journey. May you continue to flourish, finding beauty in the everyday, strength in your challenges, and joy in the present moment. Remember, you have the power to create a fulfilling and meaningful life. Embrace it fully and let your spirit shine.

Copyright © 2024 Narrato Insights LLC. All rights reserved.

Echoes of Unity:
Poems of Hope, Inspiration, Progress, and Pride

for the BIPOC Community

Narrato Insights

INTRODUCTION

Welcome to " **Echoes of Unity: Poems of Hope, Inspiration, Progress, and Pride for the BIPOC Community"** a collection of 75 poems that celebrate the rich tapestry of experiences, struggles, and triumphs of the Black, Indigenous, and People of Color community. This anthology is a tribute to the enduring spirit and boundless resilience that define us, capturing the essence of hope, progress, and pride in every verse.

In this book, you will find a diverse array of voices and perspectives, each poem uniquely titled and crafted to resonate with readers from all backgrounds. From the shadows of the past to the bright horizons of the future, these poems traverse a wide spectrum of emotions and themes. They honor the legacies of our ancestors, reflect on the challenges we face today, and envision a future where unity and love prevail.

Our journey begins with "Rising Sun," a poem that symbolizes the dawn of new possibilities and the power of collective strength. As you turn each page, you will encounter "Seeds of Change," "Voices Unbound," and "Colors of Unity," among many others, each offering a unique glimpse into the heart and soul of our community.

" **Echoes of Unity: Poems of Hope, Inspiration, Progress, and Pride for the BIPOC Community"** is more than just a collection of poems; it is a call to action and a source of inspiration. It is a reminder that despite the obstacles we face, we possess an unyielding hope and an unbreakable bond. These poems are meant to uplift, empower, and remind us of the beauty and strength that lies within each of us.

Whether you are seeking solace in difficult times, inspiration to fuel your journey, or a celebration of your heritage, this anthology offers something for everyone. Let the words within these pages be a beacon of light and a testament to the enduring spirit of the Black, Indigenous, and People of Color community.

Thank you for joining us on this journey of hope, inspiration, progress, and pride. May " **Echoes of Unity: Poems of Hope,**

Inspiration, Progress, and Pride for the BIPOC Community " touch your heart, ignite your spirit, and inspire you to carry forward the legacy of those who came before us.

Rising Sun

From shadows deep, we rise anew,
With dreams alight, our path is true.
In unity, we find our way,
Together strong, we greet the day.

Echoes of Heritage

In whispers of the past, we hear,
The strength of those who brought us here.
Their legacy, our guiding light,
We honor them with all our might.

Seeds of Change

In fertile ground, we plant our dreams,
With hope that flows in endless streams.
Each step we take, each hand we hold,
We shape a future bright and bold.

Voices Unbound

We sing our songs, both loud and clear,
Our stories echo far and near.
In every note, in every word,
Our voices rise, our truths are heard.

Colors of Unity

In shades of brown, and black, and gold,

A tapestry of lives unfolds.

In every hue, in every shade,

A vibrant world of love is made.

Strength in Struggles

From trials faced, we draw our strength,

In every fight, we've gone the length.

With heads held high, we stand our ground,

In unity, our power's found.

Future's Promise

The future calls, a beacon bright,

With dreams that fill the darkest night.

Together, we will forge ahead,

With hope and love, our path is spread.

Legacy of Love

In hearts that beat with love and pride,

We carry forth those who have died.

Their spirits guide us every day,

In love's embrace, we find our way.

Unyielding Hope

In every dawn, a promise lies,
A chance to reach and touch the skies.
With hope as our eternal guide,
We walk with strength, with love and pride.

Dreamers Awake

We dream of worlds where we are free,
Where every soul can truly be.
In every dream, a seed is sown,
A world of love, where we are known.

Courageous Hearts

In every heart that beats with fire,
We find the strength to reach higher.
With courage bold, we face each day,
In unity, we find our way.

Pathways to Progress

In every step, in every stride,
We move with hope and boundless pride.
With every goal, with every gain,
We honor those who broke the chain.

Dawn's Embrace

As dawn breaks through the darkest night,
We find our way, we seek the light.
In every ray, in every beam,
We see the hope, we live the dream.

Resilient Spirits

In every challenge, we remain,
With spirits strong, we bear the pain.
In every trial, in every test,
We rise again, we do our best.

Winds of Change

The winds of change are blowing strong,
With hope and love, we sing our song.
In every breeze, in every gust,
We find the strength, in love we trust.

United We Stand

In unity, we find our might,
Together strong, we face the fight.
With hearts aligned, with spirits free,
We walk the path to victory.

Horizons of Hope

In distant lands, in skies so wide,

We see the hope, we feel the pride.

With every step, with every stride,

We move ahead, with love as our guide.

Shades of Strength

In every shade, in every hue,

A story told, a journey true.

With strength we rise, with pride we stand,

A united, diverse, and vibrant land.

Bridges of Love

We build our bridges strong and wide,

With love and hope, we walk with pride.

In every step, in every leap,

We find the dreams that we will keep.

Echoes of Triumph

From battles fought, from victories won,

We stand as one, beneath the sun.

With every cheer, with every cry,

We honor those who did not die.

Blossoms of Tomorrow

In every bud, a promise lies,

A future bright before our eyes.

With tender care, with love's embrace,

We nurture dreams in every place.

Voices of Victory

In every voice that shouts with pride,

We hear the tales of those who tried.

In every song, in every cheer,

We find the strength to persevere.

Pillars of Progress

In every step towards the light,

We build the world with all our might.

With every stone, with every brick,

We lay the path both sure and thick.

Rainbow of Dreams

In every color, in every shade,

A future bright and unafraid.

With every dream, with every goal,

We find the strength within our soul.

Unbroken Chains

From chains unbound, we rise anew,

With strength in hearts and dreams in view.

In unity, our future lies,

With hope and love, we touch the skies.

Heartbeats of Hope

In every heartbeat, strong and true,

We find the strength to start anew.

With every beat, with every pulse,

We move ahead, we feel the rush.

Songs of Freedom

We sing the songs of freedom's light,
With voices strong, we claim our right.
In every note, in every tune,
We celebrate, we rise, we bloom.

Dreams of Unity

In dreams of unity, we see,
A world where we are truly free.
With hearts aligned, with spirits high,
We reach for stars beyond the sky.

Waves of Progress

In waves of progress, we ascend,

With hope and love, our guide and friend.

In every crest, in every trough,

We find the strength, we are enough.

Fires of Hope

In fires of hope, we burn so bright,

With dreams that pierce the darkest night.

In every flame, in every spark,

We find the strength to leave our mark.

<u>Bonds of Love</u>

In bonds of love, we find our way,
Together strong, we face the day.
In every hug, in every touch,
We feel the hope, we feel so much.

<u>Dreams Reborn</u>

In dreams reborn, we find our peace,
A future bright, a world at ease.
With every dream, with every plan,
We build the world with our own hand.

Pathways of Light

In pathways of light, we find our way,
With hope that guides us every day.
In every step, in every stride,
We move with love, with endless pride.

Blossoms of Unity

In every blossom, bright and fair,
We see the love we all can share.
With every petal, soft and true,
We build a world that's born anew.

<u>Triumphs of the Heart</u>

In triumphs of the heart, we rise,

With dreams that reach beyond the skies.

In every beat, in every cheer,

We find the hope that conquers fear.

<u>Rays of Hope</u>

In rays of hope, we find our strength,

With dreams that stretch beyond the length.

In every beam, in every light,

We see a future bold and bright.

<u>Songs of Tomorrow</u>

We sing the songs of what's to come,

With hearts that beat like a drum.

In every note, in every rhyme,

We move ahead, we find our time.

<u>Dreams of Strength</u>

In dreams of strength, we find our way,

With courage bold, we greet the day.

In every dream, in every goal,

We find the strength within our soul.

<u>Blossoms of Pride</u>

In every blossom, bright and fair,

We see the pride we all can share.

With every petal, soft and true,

We build a world that's born anew.

<u>Bridges of Hope</u>

We build our bridges strong and wide,

With love and hope, we walk with pride.

In every step, in every leap,

We find the dreams that we will keep.

<u>Winds of Unity</u>

The winds of unity blow strong,
With hope and love, we sing our song.
In every breeze, in every gust,
We find the strength, in love we trust.

<u>Echoes of Love</u>

In echoes of love, we find our peace,
A future bright, a world at ease.
With every word, with every sound,
We build a world where love is found.

<u>Dreams of Progress</u>

In dreams of progress, we ascend,

With hope and love, our guide and friend.

In every dream, in every plan,

We build the world with our own hand.

<u>Hearts of Hope</u>

In hearts of hope, we find our way,

Together strong, we face the day.

In every beat, in every touch,

We feel the hope, we feel so much.

<u>Voices of Hope</u>

In every voice that shouts with pride,
We hear the tales of those who tried.
In every song, in every cheer,
We find the strength to persevere.

<u>Colors of Hope</u>

In shades of brown, and black, and gold,
A tapestry of lives unfolds.
In every hue, in every shade,
A vibrant world of love is made.

Dreams of Love

In dreams of love, we find our peace,
A future bright, a world at ease.
With every dream, with every plan,
We build the world with our own hand.

Pathways of Hope

In pathways of hope, we find our way,
With love that guides us every day.
In every step, in every stride,
We move with pride, with endless hope.

<u>Triumphs of Unity</u>

In triumphs of unity, we rise,
With dreams that reach beyond the skies.
In every beat, in every cheer,
We find the hope that conquers fear.

<u>SEEDS OF UNITY</u>

In fertile ground, we plant our dreams,
With hope that flows in endless streams.
Each step we take, each hand we hold,
We shape a future bright and bold.

<u>Threads of Unity</u>

In every thread that weaves our tale,
We find the strength to never fail.
With hands entwined, with hearts so pure,
In unity, we shall endure.

<u>Journey of Hope</u>

In every step of our long trek,
We carry dreams upon our neck.
With hope as our eternal guide,
We walk with courage, side by side.

<u>Guardians of Tomorrow</u>

We stand as guardians of tomorrow,

With hearts that beat through joy and sorrow.

In every dawn, a future bright,

We light the way, we chase the night.

<u>Harmonies of Love</u>

In harmonies that fill the air,

We find a love beyond compare.

With every note, with every song,

We build a world where we belong.

Pillars of Dreams

In pillars strong, our dreams reside,
With hope and faith, they do not hide.
In every stone, in every beam,
We build a world that dares to dream.

Radiant Horizons

On radiant horizons far and wide,
We see our dreams, we feel the pride.
With every glance, with every gaze,
We light the world in endless ways.

Tides of Change

In tides that shift, we find our way,

With hope that guides us day by day.

In every wave, in every swell,

We rise anew, we cast our spell.

Unseen Bonds

In bonds unseen, our strength is found,

With love that lifts us from the ground.

In every heart, in every mind,

A world of dreams, a love that binds.

Songs of Triumph

We sing the songs of triumph loud,

With voices strong and spirits proud.

In every cheer, in every cry,

We reach the stars, we touch the sky.

Bridges of Dreams

We build our bridges firm and wide,

With love and hope, we stride with pride.

In every span, in every link,

We forge a future bold and pink.

<u>Waves of Hope</u>

In waves of hope, we find our grace,

With dreams that light the darkest space.

In every crest, in every trough,

We find the strength, we are enough.

<u>Blossoms of Strength</u>

In every blossom bright and fair,

We see the strength we all can share.

With every petal, soft and true,

We build a world that's born anew.

Dreams of Light

In dreams of light, we find our way,
With hope that guides us every day.
In every dream, in every night,
We see the future shining bright.

Echoes of Love

In echoes of love, we find our peace,
A future bright, a world at ease.
With every word, with every sound,
We build a world where love is found.

<u>Voices of Strength</u>

In every voice that shouts with pride,
We hear the tales of those who tried.
In every song, in every cheer,
We find the strength to persevere.

<u>Winds of Unity</u>

The winds of unity blow strong,
With hope and love, we sing our song.
In every breeze, in every gust,
We find the strength, in love we trust.

Seeds of Progress

In fertile ground, we plant our dreams,
With hope that flows in endless streams.
Each step we take, each hand we hold,
We shape a future bright and bold.

Dreamers Arise

We dream of worlds where we are free,
Where every soul can truly be.
In every dream, a seed is sown,
A world of love, where we are known.

Heartbeats of Unity

In every heartbeat, strong and true,
We find the strength to start anew.
With every beat, with every pulse,
We move ahead, we feel the rush.

Rays of Promise

In rays of promise, we find our light,
With dreams that pierce the darkest night.
In every beam, in every ray,
We see a future bold and gay.

Colors of Progress

In every shade, in every hue,

A story told, a journey true.

With strength we rise, with pride we stand,

A united, diverse, and vibrant land.

Harmonies of Progress

In harmonies that blend so sweet,

We find the progress at our feet.

With every chord, with every tune,

We build a world that dares to bloom.

Dreams of Tomorrow

In dreams of tomorrow, we ascend,
With hope and love, our guide and friend.
In every dream, in every plan,
We build the world with our own hand.

Bonds of Progress

In bonds of progress, we unite,
Together strong, we face the fight.
With hearts aligned, with spirits free,
We walk the path to victory.

Future's Harmony

The future sings a song so bright,
With dreams that fill the darkest night.
Together, we will forge ahead,
With hope and love, our path is spread.

Conclusion

As we reach the end of " **Echoes of Unity: Poems of Hope, Inspiration, Progress, and Pride for the BIPOC Community**," we reflect on the journey we have taken through the vibrant and powerful tapestry of poems that celebrate the Black, Indigenous, and People of Color community. Each poem, a testament to the strength, resilience, and unbreakable spirit of our people, has painted a picture of hope, progress, and pride.

These verses have transported us through the whispers of heritage, the struggles of the present, and the dreams of the future. They have reminded us of the importance of unity, the power of our collective voices, and the beauty of our diverse experiences. In every line, we have felt the echoes of our shared history and the promise of a brighter tomorrow.

The journey through these poems is a reminder that we are not alone. We are part of a larger community, a powerful force of love and strength that spans generations and borders. Our stories, our dreams, and our voices are interwoven into a rich and vibrant tapestry that continues to grow and evolve.

As you close this book, carry with you the messages of hope and inspiration found within its pages. Let them guide you, uplift you, and remind you of the beauty and power that lies within you. Share these poems with others, and let their words inspire change, unity, and progress in your own community.

" **Echoes of Unity: Poems of Hope, Inspiration, Progress, and Pride for the BIPOC Community** " is more than just a collection of poems; it is a celebration of our shared journey and a testament to our collective strength. It is a beacon of light in times of darkness and a source of pride in times of triumph.

Thank you for joining us on this journey. May the echoes of unity continue to resonate in your heart, and may the spirit of hope, progress, and pride guide you always.

Anthology Conclusion

As you close this anthology, take a moment to reflect on the journey you've just experienced. The poems within **Resilient Voices: A Poetry Anthology** are more than mere words on a page—they are echoes of our shared humanity, reminders of the strength we all possess, and beacons of hope in times of darkness.

In these pages, we have explored the depths of sorrow and the heights of joy. We have walked through valleys of despair and stood on peaks of triumph. Each poem has been a testament to the resilience that lies within us all, a celebration of the unyielding spirit that keeps us moving forward, no matter the obstacles we face.

The voices you've heard in this collection are not just the voices of poets—they are the voices of every person who has ever faced a challenge and found the courage to rise again. They are your voice, speaking to your heart, reminding you that you are not alone on this journey.

As you step back into the world, carry with you the messages of strength, hope, and resilience that *Resilient Voices* offers. Let these poems be a source of comfort in difficult times, a wellspring of inspiration when you need it most, and a reminder that within you lies the power to overcome anything.

Thank you for joining us on this poetic journey. May the words you've encountered here continue to inspire you, uplift you, and remind you of the beauty and strength that reside within every mind and heart.